Learning to Read, Step by Step!

Ready to Read   Preschool–Kindergarten
• big type and easy words • rhyme and rhythm • picture clues
For children who know the alphabet and are eager to
begin reading.

Reading with Help   Preschool–Grade 1
• basic vocabulary • short sentences • simple stories
For children who recognize familiar words and sound out
new words with help.

Reading on Your Own   Grades 1–3
• engaging characters • easy-to-follow plots • popular topics
For children who are ready to read on their own.

Reading Paragraphs   Grades 2–3
• challenging vocabulary • short paragraphs • exciting stories
For newly independent readers who read simple sentences
with confidence.

Ready for Chapters   Grades 2–4
• chapters • longer paragraphs • full-color art
For children who want to take the plunge into chapter books
but still like colorful pictures.

STEP INTO READING® is designed to give every child a successful
reading experience. The grade levels are only guides; children will progress
through the steps at their own speed, developing confidence in their reading.
The F&P Text Level on the back cover serves as another tool to help you
choose the right book for your child.

Remember, a lifetime love of reading starts with a single step!

To Bethany Perl,
with a big toothy grin! —E.S.P.

To Lily, who always finds the truth —M.S.

Acknowledgments: The author and editor gratefully acknowledge the help of Marie Levine, Executive Director of the Shark Research Institute (sharks.org); Jillian Morris, Founder and President of Sharks4Kids (sharks4kids.com); and Masa Ushioda of SeaPics (seapics.com). Thank you very much!

Photograph credits: Cover photograph © Doug Perrine/SeaPics.com; p. 3 © James D. Watt/ SeaPics.com; p. 4 (top) © Espen Rekdal/SeaPics.com, (bottom) © James D. Watt/SeaPics.com; p. 5 (left) © Mark Conlin/SeaPics.com, (right) © C & M Fallows/SeaPics.com; p. 8 (top) © Andy Murch/ SeaPics.com, (bottom) © Mark Strickland/SeaPics.com; p. 9 (top) © James D. Watt/SeaPics.com, (bottom) © Howard Hall/SeaPics.com; p. 13 © Will Schubert/SeaPics.com; p. 16 © Doug Perrine/ SeaPics.com; p. 17 © Masakazu Ushioda/SeaPics.com; p. 20 © Masakazu Ushioda/SeaPics.com; p. 21 (top) © Andy Murch/SeaPics.com, (bottom) © Andy Murch/SeaPics.com; pp. 24–25 © Phillip Colla/ SeaPics.com; p. 28 © D. R. Schrichte/SeaPics.com; p. 29 (top) © Gwen Lowe/SeaPics.com, (bottom) © David Shen/SeaPics.com; p. 32 © Chris Huss/SeaPics.com; p. 33 (left) © Martin Strmiska/ SeaPics.com, (right) © Masakazu Ushioda/SeaPics.com; p. 36 © Marty Snyderman/SeaPics.com; p. 37 © Doc White/SeaPics.com; p. 41 © Nobuo Kitagawa/e-Photo/SeaPics.com; p. 45 (top & bottom) © Duncan Brake/Sharks4Kids

Library of Congress Cataloging-in-Publication Data is available upon request.
ISBN 978-0-525-57879-6 (pbk.) — ISBN 978-0-525-57880-2 (lib. bdg.) — ISBN 978-0-525-57881-9 (ebook)

Printed in the United States of America
10 9 8 7 6 5 4 3 2 1

This book has been officially leveled by using the F&P Text Level Gradient™ Leveling System.

TRUTH or LIE
SHARKS!

by Erica S. Perl

illustrations by Michael Slack

Random House 🏠 New York

Hi! I'm the TRUTH SLEUTH. Look at all these sharks! There are over four hundred kinds of sharks, from the dwarf lantern shark to the whale shark.

Tiny!

Dwarf lantern shark

Huge!

Whale shark

It's TRUE!

But I smell a LIE nearby.

Let's play TRUTH OR LIE

and find it!

When you turn the page,

you'll see four statements . . .

BUT only three are TRUE.

Hammerhead shark

Great white shark

Which one is a LIE?

Take a guess!

1. Some baby sharks hatch from eggs, just like baby birds.

2. Some mother sharks give birth to live babies, just like mother dolphins.

3. Baby sharks are toothless at first.

4. Baby sharks take care of themselves right away.

The lie is . . .

3. Baby sharks are toothless at first.

Baby sharks have teeth
when they are born.
They need to take care of
themselves right away.
They catch their own dinner.

Shortfin mako shark

Silvertip shark, juvenile and adu

And they protect themselves

so they don't become

someone else's dinner!

Tiger shark, juvenile and adult

Baby swell shark coming out of egg case

See if you can find the LIE here.

1. A shark's skin is armored.

2. Sharks do not shed their skin.

3. Many sharks have

    darker skin on their backs

    and paler skin on their bellies.

4. A shark's skin is easily cut.

The lie is . . .

4. A shark's skin is easily cut.

Not true,

because the skin

of a shark is very tough.

It is covered with denticles

(say DENT-uh-kulz).

Denticles are tough scales.

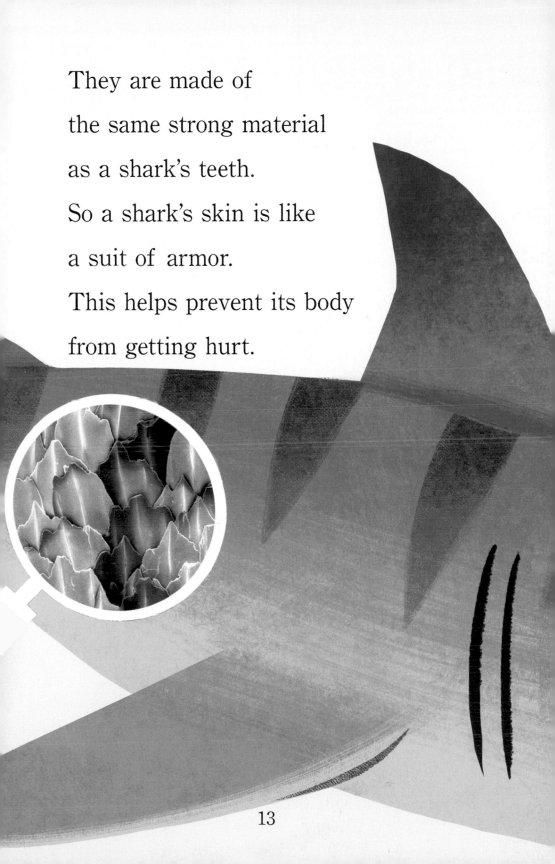

They are made of
the same strong material
as a shark's teeth.
So a shark's skin is like
a suit of armor.
This helps prevent its body
from getting hurt.

1. Sharks have eyes but no ears.

2. Sharks have eyes and ears.

3. Sharks have eyes and ears and gills.

4. People have eyes and ears
but no gills.

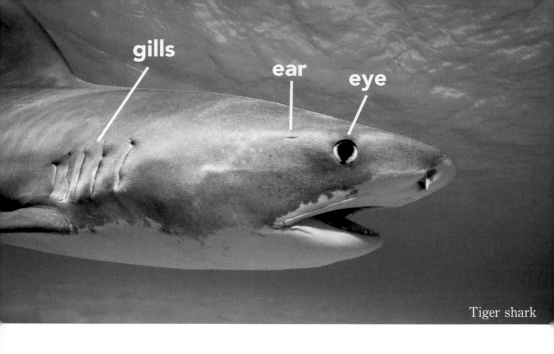

gills

ear

eye

Tiger shark

The lie is . . .

1. Sharks have eyes but no ears.

You can easily see
a shark's eyes and gills.
But a shark's ears
are inside its head,
through two small openings
on either side.

Sharks also have another way
to "hear" movement.
Special pores along their bodies
detect vibrations in the water.
So never try to sneak up
on a shark!

pores

Caribbean reef shark

17

Let's try another.

Which is the LIE?

1. Sharks have skeletons.

2. A shark skeleton is made of bones.

3. People have more bones
   than sharks.

4. A shark does not have
   a funny bone.

X-RAY

The lie is . . .

2. A shark skeleton is made of bones.

Sharks don't have any bones,

not even a funny bone!

A shark skeleton

is made of cartilage.

Cartilage is lighter

and more bendable than bone.

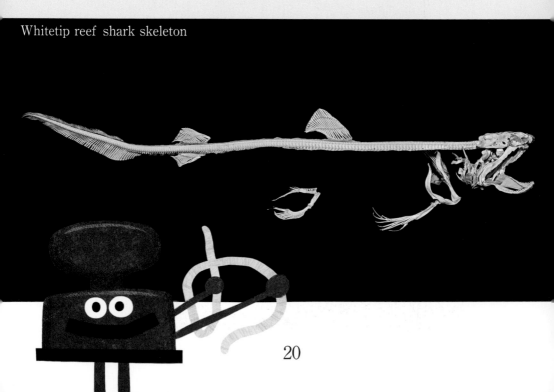

Whitetip reef shark skeleton

Hammerhead shark

This gives many sharks,

like the shortfin mako shark,

the flexibility that helps them

swim and turn so fast.

Shortfin mako shark

21

1. The dorsal fin is a kind of shark fin.

2. The pectoral fin is a kind of
   shark fin.

3. The puff fin is a kind of shark fin.

4. The caudal fin is a kind of shark fin.

The lie is . . .

3. The puff fin is a kind of shark fin.

A shark doesn't have a "puff fin."
But a shark does have
several kinds of fins,
each with a different job.
A shark uses its caudal fin
(or tail fin) to propel itself
through the water.

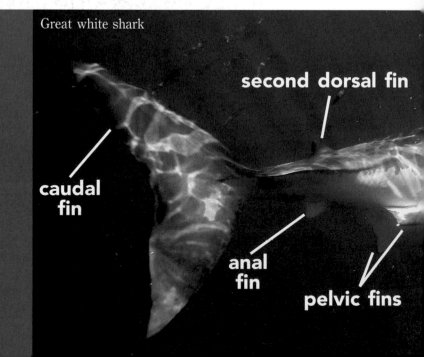

Great white shark

second dorsal fin

caudal
fin

anal
fin

pelvic fins

Pectoral fins are for
steering.
Dorsal fins help in making
sudden turns.
The pelvic and anal fins
are used for stability.
The shape and position
of a shark's fins can tell us
where it lives
and how it hunts.

first dorsal fin

pectoral fins

Puff fin—get it?
Puffin! See, *I* have
a funny bone!

My, what a big LIE!

Can you find it?

1. The goblin shark can shoot its jaws forward when it bites.
2. The cookie-cutter shark takes cookie-shaped bites from its prey.
3. A shark's jaws are not attached to its skull.
4. Sharks rarely lose teeth.

Have you seen my teeth?

The lie is . . .

4. Sharks rarely lose teeth.

Sharks actually lose and replace

their teeth constantly.

Some go through

up to fifty thousand teeth

in a lifetime!

Sand tiger shark

Have you ever lost a tooth
while biting into an apple?
Just like you,
sharks can lose teeth
when chomping into a meal.
And some sharks
(like the goblin shark
and the cookie-cutter shark)
have very unusual ways
of chomping!

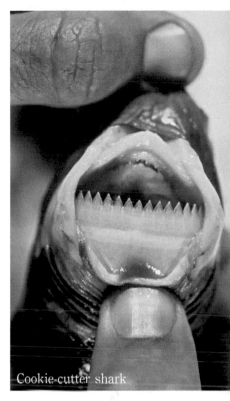

Cookie-cutter shark

Goblin shark

Can you nail down a LIE about hammerhead sharks?

1. This shark's name comes from the shape of its head.
2. Hammerhead sharks often swim with screwdriver sharks.
3. Hammerhead sharks have special sensors on their heads that help them find food.
4. The hammerhead shark's favorite food is stingrays.

The lie is . . .

2. Hammerhead sharks often swim with screwdriver sharks.

Screwdriver sharks don't exist,
but hammerhead sharks do.

Their unusual head shape,

eye position,

and special sensors

help them hunt for food

hidden in the sand.

I spy another LIE nearby.

1. The biggest shark is the whale shark.
2. The whale shark is bigger than a school bus.
3. The whale shark is not a whale.
4. The whale shark is dangerous to people.

The lie is . . .

4. The whale shark is dangerous to people.

Whale sharks
are the biggest sharks.
Some are up to forty feet long!
But they are gentle giants.

They swim with their
huge mouths open
to collect tiny animals and plants
called plankton.
Each day,
a whale shark can eat at least
fifty pounds of plankton.

Can you uncover the LIE here?

1. All sharks need to swim constantly in order to breathe.

2. Sharks breathe through slits called gills.

3. Most sharks have five gill slits on each side of their head.

4. Some sharks have seven gill slits on each side of their head.

The lie is . . .

1. All sharks need to swim constantly in order to breathe.

People breathe air,

but sharks breathe water

through their gills.

It's true some kinds of sharks

must always swim

in order to keep water moving

through their gills.

But other sharks have
small openings behind their eyes
called spiracles (say SPEER-uh-kulz).
Spiracles force water
across these sharks' gills
so they can still breathe
while they rest.

Zebra shark

spiracle

See if you can spot our final LIE.
Every year . . .

1. More people are injured by toilets than by sharks.

2. More people are injured by lightning than by sharks.

3. More people are injured by fireworks than by sharks.

4. More people are injured by sharks than sharks are injured by people.

The lie is . . .

4. More people are injured by sharks than sharks are injured by people.

Fewer than one hundred people
are injured by sharks each year.
Between seventy-three million and
one hundred million sharks
are killed by people each year!
Scientists and activists
are trying to reduce that number
by showing how sharks
keep our oceans healthy.

You did it!
You are officially a
TRUTH SLEUTH, too.
Keep up the good work!

TRUTH
SLEUTH

- Read with an eye for TRUTH and a nose for LIES.
- Share what you know *and* how you figured out it was TRUE.
- Ask your parents, guardian, teacher, or librarian to help you find the best books and most reliable websites.
- Play TRUTH OR LIE with your friends and family.

Want to Learn More FACTS About Sharks?

Books to read:

The Great White Shark Scientist by Sy Montgomery
(Houghton Mifflin Harcourt, 2016)

Hungry, Hungry Sharks! by Joanna Cole (Random House
Children's Books, 1986)

*Neighborhood Sharks: Hunting with the Great Whites of
California's Farallon Islands* by Katherine Roy (Roaring
Brook Press, 2014)

Shark Lady by Jess Keating (Sourcebooks Jabberwocky, 2017)

Websites to check out:

oceana.org

sharks4kids.com

sharks.org

supportoursharks.com